# Stars Unseen

POETRY BOOKS BY GREG WATSON

*Stars Unseen* (2024)
*The Days Between* (2024)
*The Sound of Light* (2022)
*All the World at Once: New and Selected Poems* (2015)
*What Music Remains* (2011)
*The Distance Between Two Hands* (2008)
*Things You Will Never See Again* (2006)
*Pale Light from a Distant Room* (2004)
*Cold Water Memory* (2001)
*Annmarie Revisions* (2000)
*Open Door, Open Wall* (1998)


*The Road by Heart: Poems of Fatherhood* (2018)
edited by Greg Watson and Richard Broderick

# Stars Unseen

*Poems by*

GREG WATSON

HOLY COW! PRESS
Duluth, Minnesota
2024

Printed and bound in the United States.
First printing, Summer, 2024.
10 9 8 7 6 5 4 3 2 1

Library of Congress Cataloging-in-Publication Data
Watson, Greg, 1970- author.
Stars unseen : poems / Greg Watson.
First edition. | Duluth, Minnesota : Holy Cow! Press 2024.
LCCN 2024006646 | ISBN 9781666406917 (trade paperback)
LCGFT: Poetry.
LCC PS3623.A8723 S73 2024 | DDC 811/.54--dc23/eng/20240216
LC record available at https://lccn.loc.gov/2024006646

Holy Cow! Press projects are funded in part by grant awards from the
Ben and Jeanne Overman Charitable Trust, the Elmer L. and Eleanor J.
Andersen Foundation, the Lenfestey Family Foundation, the Woessner
Freeman Family Foundation and by gifts from generous individual
donors. We are grateful to Springboard for the Arts for their support as
our fiscal sponsor.

Holy Cow! Press books are distributed to the trade by Consortium Book
Sales & Distribution, c/o Ingram Publisher Services, Inc., 210 American
Drive, Jackson, TN 38301.

For inquiries, please write to: *Holy Cow! Press*, Post Office Box 3170, Mount
Royal Station, Duluth, MN 55803.
Visit *www.holycowpress.org*

*for my family,*

*past, present, and future*

# Contents

"I think I'll keep on describing things
to ensure that they really happened."

—Stephen Dunn

I

# Storm

We are staying up late, my young daughter
and I, to watch and listen – sleepy
though we are – to the summer lightning
storm outside, which flashes, matchstick quick
and seemingly at random, across each
small window of the flimsy French doors.
This light show is more exhilarating
to her than the storybooks stacked beside us,
which wait patiently until the world
becomes once more calm and ordinary,
in need of retelling, embellishment, magic.
For now, we wait, counting out loud
the seconds between flicker and crash,
the dark shoulders of trees and angled outlines
of rooftops, lit up for a moment, then gone.
When we startle, it is merely with delight.
We do not speak – not now, not today–
of the horrors on the television news,
the once unimaginable now commonplace,
school children crouched under desks,
their backpacks cradled close, utilized as shields
against a hail of bullets from every direction.
For now, the danger is less specific;
for now, we are snug and secure in this
boat of a bed, letting the wild, wind-swept
currents surrounding us have their say,
our small, indeterminate patch of the universe
throwing off sparks, shifting, nearly breaking apart,
reminding us of all that we live within.
When the storm at last seems spent,

I rise to close the curtains, our plastic moon
of a nightlight standing in for the one
which we cannot see. But we know it's there,
as the stars are there, and the faraway sun
of tomorrow, like all good things,
and it's enough – for now, for now –
to rest, at ease, in that simple knowing.

# Finnish Funeral, Aitkin, Minnesota (1939)

It's impossible to know who is behind
the camera's clicking shutter, capturing these
mourners gathered beneath a haze
of summer sun, in somber black and gray,
gazing, without exception, at the dry ground.
Not so unusual, perhaps, for a people
known for their stoicism, for not making such
a fuss about this life, whose language offers
many words to describe the existential weight
of snow and ice, but lacks all future tense.
The pallbearers stand on the back of the flatbed,
the hand-carved coffin between them,
men long accustomed to labor, not quite
prepared for this task, their faces shadowed
by grief, hands held close to their bodies,
as if already clutching at bits of earth.
My father is the baby here, knowing only
his own hunger, memorizing each face,
the sound of their voices, each particular touch,
while my mother, many miles away, has not
yet opened her blue eyes to this world.
My great-grandmother is about to be carried,
slowly, just outside of the picture frame,
becoming, within that moment, part of what
we call history, that lengthening shadow
with which we travel, though never quite
manage to catch up with, that which
shows no sign of stopping for us,
or even slowing down.

# Saying Grace

When we were kids, we folded our
small peasant hands, freshly washed with
Ivory soap, into imaginary cathedrals,
reciting the humble words as instructed
to our invisible father, his earthly son,
and – most mysterious of all – a ghost which
we could only presume to be benevolent.
We prayed in earnest, though sometimes
in haste or with a decidedly unwelcome humor,
prayed beneath that familiar painting
which every home seemed to have in those days –
that of an old man, also in prayer, visibly weary
yet grateful for his daily crust of bread.
He seemed somehow holy to me,
and yet as earthly and ordinary as any of us.
I sometimes wondered if he might offer
up a word or two on behalf of us
poor sinners, who always seemed on the cusp
of eviction, of fleeing again by cover
of night, our offerings too small to be noticed,
our debts to the Lord, and to those who
claimed to be in his service, unpaid.

# GHAZAL LOOKING EAST, THEN WEST

I come from a people whose language has no future tense,
where love itself is measured simply by standing still.

My mother's ancestors brought bad habits but good songs,
their thirsty ghosts lingering around the whiskey still.

You told me once that loyalty was a defect of character.
My heart is a three-legged dog following you still.

Perhaps it's not love if something doesn't get broken.
When everything shatters, even the world becomes still.

My daughter spotted a dolphin in the Mississippi last week.
A child's eye can do that, can hold a great river still.

We listen closely to the arguments of winter crows,
the air between each shriek growing all the more still.

My thoughts weren't all that interesting, so I let them go.
They wore themselves out, pretending to be still.

# My Mother's Guitar

My mother's guitar, gone silent now
these past few years, rests in a corner of the room,
behind that old worn chair, each of them
weary, each leaning in their separate directions.
I remember clearly the first songs
it offered up: *Froggy Went A-Courtin'*,
*Blowin' in the Wind*, *The Wayfaring Stranger*;
remember, too, the warm, earthy smell
inside its Bible-black case, the ghost image
of its six strings in that gold plush lining,
long, thin roads disappearing into themselves.
I can see the wooden cathedral hidden
deep within its sound hole, small sparks
of angled light drifting in and out of view.
The hands that made those chords ring have
flown like birds, far away, hands gone
arthritic, fingers alternately tingling and numb.
But I can still feel the fine ridges wrapped
around each string, how the smallest touch
sounded like a secret being whispered,
a kind of conjuring with no need for words.
It rests here now, between journeys, exhaling
nearly audibly, holding its songs closely,
forever patient in its memories, its history,
its knowing, not forgetting the breath
and blood that rose imperceptibly to meet it,
not letting go of any of it. Not just yet.

# THE BUGGY

You won't remember now being quite
so small, combing that long stretch of Carolina
sand for rocks, shells, anything shining,
the ocean insistently whispering its secret
language, untranslatable upon land.
Nor will you recall the wheels of your stroller
edging closer and closer to the waves,
so slowly that none of us took notice,
none but that stout Eastern European woman
in head scarf, waving her thick arms,
shouting in alarm, "The buggy! The buggy!"
For one flashing moment, my heart leapt
like a startled fish, believing she might actually
be right, that you might be spirited away
by the unforgiving Atlantic, to Scotland
or Wales, those fabled white cliffs of Dover,
closer to your family's ancestral home
but further from the ones who love you here.
But, of course, you were right there
when we turned to look, your beach hat
shielding your eyes, your chubby legs
just beginning to learn what they're for,
ready, soon enough, to carry you anywhere.

# Illness During Childhood

When my daughter becomes sick with fever,
unable to keep even water down, I am taken back
suddenly to those terrible illnesses of childhood,
gathering like storms on the horizons of
our brows, all of us, heat blazing through temples
east and west. I remember the holy eucharist
of saltines and warm 7-Up, the pinpricks of pleurisy
through lungs gone weary with coughing,
throat scraped raw, red one day, spotted white
the next, giving up the ghost of speech;
remember, too, the little brown bottles of Robitussin,
the mountains of knotted tissue hardening,
the smell of sickness seeping into everything.
I am reminded of how we learned to walk
through sleep, as we had in waking life, pushing
hard in our delirium against heavy furniture
as though ships stubbornly clinging to shore,
while visions of saints and ancestors floated patiently
past our doors and windows, visitors which no one
would have believed had we mentioned them.
I remember how we became somehow weightless
and immovable at once, sleeping so hard
that no dream could have roused us, our limbs
growing limp and longer through the night,
reaching out for that mythical land of sunlight
and well being, until one morning we did
awake, bright-eyed once more upon a shore
of cool linoleum, our bodies new and uncertain,
flat feet plodding from one room to the next,
so thirsty we could have drunk the rain clouds dry.

# MOTHER AND CHILD

Just across the street, where yet another
sleek, modern apartment complex has miraculously
arisen overnight, I can spy the figure
of a woman in one window, many stories up,
gently swaying, her baby blanketed and held closely,
moving perhaps to a music which only they
can hear, or to the silence they share between
them, framed within this moment, far above
the groans of winter traffic below, a maddening
wind rushing the clouds along, rattling the
tiny metal doors of street lamps and flagpoles,
bending the trees one way, then another.
I look away, only for a moment, and of course
they are gone, the window glass shimmering with
winter blues, an amber-tinted light bulb
reflected like a distant star, slowly receding
from view on such a cold and bitter morning,
just now beginning to stir, just now
beginning to wake into the story of itself.

# My Daughter Speaks of Birds

My daughter speaks of birds, speaks in wonder
of their sing-song call and response,
their endless reserve of resilience and guile
in the face of all manner of adversity,
the sudden and startling grace of their flight,
which, after all this time, continues to
amaze those of us standing
flat-footed on the earth below.

She asks which bird I might come back as
after I have departed from this life,
and how she will know it's me.
"Fly close to me three times," she suggests,
"then give out one call." This seems
a reasonable request, provided my new
bird-self can remember the details.

Our ancestors, after all, believed that
the soul was carried in, and away,
on the wings of the *sielulintu**,
that the whole earth and sky were formed
from the cracked shell of a fallen egg.
We settle, for now, upon a common jay,
brightly handsome but unassuming,
vigilant in watching over its family, never
straying far from its wooded home.

We have, I hope, the better part of this life
to draw our fragile maps, to practice
and perfect our signals, our language
of mutual understanding.

---

* *sielulintu* – "soul bird" (Finnish)

# Soap

God only knows what casual blasphemy
or stubborn refusal of a chore had tumbled out,
but there I was, a child of four, made
to kneel upon the smoke-yellow linoleum
of the bathroom floor, a fresh white bar
of soap clenched between my teeth.

I was instructed to bite down, to think deeply
on my thoughts and actions, and to ask the Lord,
as I often did, for forgiveness. I cannot say
whether or not it arrived, only that
the waiting felt like hours – a thousand years
to the creator, after all, being one day.

The soap did nothing to cleanse,
nor to make what came out of me any wiser,
every uncertain lisp and stutter floating
like bubbles up toward the heavens. I tasted
only shame, resentment, a chemical bitterness
that lasted the whole length of the day.

I understood words to be weighted things,
meant to be avoided whenever possible,
and God the father, forever holding his tongue,
to be always listening, always ready
to silence with the back of a hand, a sword,
or a book thrown suddenly open.

# CANDY CIGARETTES

We bought them with the nickels
and pennies of our weekly allowance
at the Little General corner store,
tucked them hastily in small paper sacks
along with the crystal blue and amber jewels
of hard candy, the stale Tootsie Rolls,
Red Hots, and aptly named Jawbreakers.
We practiced looking tough, or just thoughtful,
practiced those mannered turns and gestures
of the wrist, flicking imaginary ashes
upon the ground, or into our open palms,
white sticks of sugar dangling from
the corners of our mouths as we spoke,
blew imaginary smoke rings toward
the blue shimmering sky, tapping one end
of the pack against the soft mounds
below our thumbs, the way we had seen
the grownups do. We learned to squint like
the stars of westerns and war movies,
rolled the crinkling packs into the shoulders
of our thin cotton tees, before setting off
on Big Wheels and bikes, the sand and
broken glass of housing project sidewalks
crunching beneath our wheels, toward a future
already being written for us, up there
amongst the shifting clouds.

# The Fawn

Walking to work through the half-dark soot of early morning, chemicals still clinging to the damp air, I am startled by the motionless gaze of a young deer, peering through the cemetery's black iron fence, solitary, unimpressed and unafraid by my presence. White mist, like the small clouds along her ribs, hovers near the ground. For the past two nights, whole blocks of this street have gone up in flames, set off by protestors or outside agitators, blackened brick and the empty easels of storefronts now waiting for whatever sunlight can break through. On the opposite side of the street, this thin-legged beauty nibbles calmly at the grass and flowers, as if saying plainly, "This land was here long before you and your dead arrived." Having satisfied her belly and curiosity, she is gone, in the flash of a single leap, an agility reserved for the eternally hunted. While I continue on, the interloper in this scene, my own awkward frame lumbering along, moving further and further out of view.

# D.a.v. Thrift Store

Another nowhere job in my early twenties was at
the D.A.V. Thrift Store on University Avenue,
unloading and pricing junk merchandise
as it rolled in off the box trucks.

Used toasters, baby strollers, bedding,
odds and ends, those old man cardigan sweaters
which I had suddenly grown fond of.
Harry, in his sixties, with black brille-creamed hair,
pencil mustache, blue-green Merchant Marine
tattoo fading into itself, chain-smoked
throughout the workday, shaking his head
in wonder at the myriad things
people were willing to buy.

He had eyes for Gina, the young blonde cashier,
doughy-faced, quiet, and disarmingly naive.
Then, there was the middle-aged man who was
permanently banned from the store
for obsessively sniffing women's shoes,
kneeling before the racks in a form of obeisance
or defeat, a grossly tragic or comedic form
of loneliness, depending on your perspective.

We were all doing time in our own way,
students, retirees, and the occasional criminal,
going nowhere on a daily basis.
Except, as it turned out, Harry and Gina,
who ran away together without notice, sending
a postcard-sized photo back months later

of no determinable location, trees bent
into question marks, and long grass waving,
sparks of blue water in the background.

"Wish you were here," was all it read.
And I would venture that every one of us,
without exception, certainly did.

# Errand

My mother had already broken the eggs,
measured out the bleached white flour, before
realizing that we were out of sugar.

Which is how I found myself – a child of seven,
hesitant to speak or approach anyone – standing at
the rusted screen door of my grandfather's
cabin with instructions to borrow a cup.

No one had mentioned this stranger before,
released from state prison to die in his own way,
away from others, like any mortally wounded animal
will do, absence being the last and only
dignity most of us can summon.

No one had warned me of the skeletal visage
which emerged, hairless and scowling,
watery blue eyes sinking deep beneath the frames
of his thick horn-rimmed glasses.

I looked down, then away. I stammered out
my small request, met merely with a cold, inscrutable
glance, bearing little or no curiosity as to my
existence, the grandson who happened to share
his date of birth, letting fall only a kind of
mumble-grunt meant to convey a simple *No*,
and a not-so-gentle closing of the door.

Only decades later did I understand why
my mother refused to go herself,

or that the instinctual, visceral fear which I felt
was, in fact, justified. But for now, I was
content enough simply to be walking away,
unconcerned with the minor failure of my mission,

while the old man receded into the confines
of self, offering only the slow certainty
of his impending departure, a bitter shadow
lengthening, imperceptible, like blood seeping
out from beneath our feet.

# Fruit Fly

I peel a Clementine tangerine for
my young daughter, and immediately,
seemingly willed into existence
from thin air, there you are, circling,
assessing, navigating the smoothest
possible surface on which to land.
No time, I suppose, for introductions,
or easing your way into a room.
Your lifetime here, after all, is so brief,
and your thirst relentless, ancestral.
Strange, then, to consider our shared DNA,
invisible ladder reaching between us,
the opposing engines of our bodies,
our separate intuitions and needs,
ostensibly whole worlds apart.
Yet you are somehow always familiar,
inventing and erasing yourself on
the shifting periphery, bumping into
the white plastered walls, as if motion
itself were the only true means
of survival, and sweetness – the very
sweetness of this world – worthy
of every possible risk.

# COUSTEAU

We liked the sound of his voice, balanced
between a child's innate wonder
and an adult's knowing, filtered through
the television's small tin speaker.
We liked his red cap bobbing against
the ever-shifting blue, his sun-weathered skin,
thin hands cradling one alien lifeform
or another, startled into being, reaching
blindly in all directions at the expanse of air.
We loved most the strangeness,
every new thing in search of a name
to match its form, this kingdom so far
removed from the certainty of classrooms,
the slate-drab housing of the projects.
How else could we have known
that the world, like us, was mostly water,
how else to imagine our small bodies
descending into darkness, unafraid,
suddenly weightless among the current,
how else could we ever have believed
in all the beauty we could not see?

# We Are Still Here

We are still here, do you understand,
standing amidst the mountains
of rubble where our children now play,

their faces reflected in the shattered glass
of storefronts and depots, the stagnant
water filling in the tracks behind you.

We have scorched the earth to ash
in order to welcome you, burned down
the humble homes our fathers built
so that you may not know their comfort.

There will be no bed for you here,
no rooms for you to enter, not a single
floorboard for you to walk upon.

For we are still here, do you understand,
singing the old songs and the new,
whistling past the graveyards you have
built as swiftly as we can fill them.

We have, you will see, made room there
for you. We are not uncivilized.
We give you seeds to fill your pockets.
We build statues of you in the snow.

We stand, you will come to know,
as the deep forest stands, unyielding,
breathing in the entirety of this sky at once.

We are still here, as even you can plainly see.
We will continue to be here until not
a single blade of grass remains,

nor a single mayfly buzzing in flight,
nothing but the breath that breathes life
into these words, however simple,
upon which we will stand, beginning anew.

# II

# ALL THE LOVE WE LAY CLAIM TO

My great-grandfather Juho leans forward slightly
in his chair, as though about to speak

or to reach out his hand one last time
to his beloved, at rest in the casket beside him,

its doorway already covered in handfuls of flowers
and soil, heavy and damp, the solemn faces

of men in the background looking on, weary,
their funeral suits and ties virtually interchangeable.

But the mourner up front wears his work shirt
for this, the hardest labor he has endured

in a lifetime of work, his hands having carved
long into the night a seemingly endless array of roses

and filigree into the wood, as he had once carved
into the marriage bed, and the children's cribs,

hands that look suddenly exposed and empty,
lingering like uncertain birds too long into winter.

Could he have imagined this moment when he arrived
from that other world, with neither currency

nor language, to stake his claim and break this
ground open like a sacred book of secrets?

He must have known, without ever having to say,
that the earth we till must be fed in return,

and all the love we lay claim to must be met equally
with grief, solid as the ground on which we stand.

This, it seems, is the only bargain we are offered,
our baffled silence continually interpreted as assent.

# CHANGING THE ENDING

How many of these old children's tales,
their yellowed pages barely clinging to the spines,
have I found myself editing and adding to
while reading to my young daughter?

How many children were spared at the last from
becoming some cretin's favorite meal,
how many kind animals saved from the axe?

What kind of mother sells her kids to the gypsies
for a handful of silver and jewels?

What kind of father could somehow be talked
into leaving his small children alone in the woods,
hungry and terrified, with only the bluebirds
and breadcrumbs to lead them home?

Even poor Francis, that inquisitive and mischievous
badger, was threatened with a spanking
for failing to fall asleep on command, with me,
grudgingly, having to explain the meaning
of the word, so foreign was the idea in our home.

Things are very different in this telling of ours,
a world apart from the one in which her father grew,
years she rightly refers to as "the olden days."

When she is older, perhaps, she may understand
how I somehow altered my own narrative,
and therefore hers as well, simply by being the father
who stayed, and who chose to do so every moment.

Though there are still days when I long to change
the story, if only by slowing it down,
pausing before the next turn of the page.

Every small moment has somehow become
my favorite, every adventure the greatest one yet.
I am only beginning to understand, dear reader,
and I confess, I never want this story to end.

# LEARNING TO LISTEN

If I am being honest, brother, my last words to you were untrue, releasing you from this life, this body, this bundle of worry in the way that I thought I was required to do. As if words mattered, mine or anyone else's, in that moment. As if you needed my permission for release. I told you that I would be alright. Another lie. I told you that I love you, words we never spoke to each other in this life. Some things, we learned early on, need not be spoken. Some things are weakened by their telling. If I am being honest, I saw no need to pray for intervention, as the others did. You were already on your way. I felt that elusive door open and close, my hand resting upon your chest, felt the air in the room shift. What could anyone say then? The silence settled in. I could only listen, in ways I am learning still.

# Fasting

Then, for reasons unclear to any of us, our mother decided that forgoing food for one day, then two, would somehow bring her children closer to God. No more sugary bowls of cereal spooned and slurped over Saturday morning cartoons, no more nuclear-orange macaroni and cheese, or chicken and dumplings simmering slowly on the stove. We were to subside instead on the spirit alone, consuming the Word like bread, dutifully reading our Bible verses out loud, mouths parched, bellies rumbling in revolt. Why, we wondered in silence, had the Creator given us bodies to nourish if we were not meant to do so? Why was He in need of constant reassurance? Was not our steadfast belief enough? We knew only the immediacy of our hunger, its gnawing persistence, our living room suddenly the proverbial wilderness of old, void of growth. We called out, like Elijah, like the Lord himself, waited for a sign or response. But we were no prophets, merely kids, our small hands trembling when at last we were allowed to break our fasts. And though the Lord felt further away than ever, we naturally said grace, said it like we meant it.

# First Apartment

When I think of being seventeen, I think
of that dingey one room walk-up above
the nameless laundromat, its dirty glass clouded
with steam, potato-sweat stench and clutter
of that windowless apartment, rickety wooden stairs
leaning wearily against the red brick outside,
ready to collapse, shifting even without the weight of steps.
I remember the anonymous maps of water-stained
walls, so thin that I could hear my neighbors
coughing and brushing their teeth, playing the same
sad songs over and over, could feel the vibrations
of the industrial washers and dryers below, like invisible
lovers nearing climax, never quite arriving.
When I think of being seventeen, I think
of walking to school in the dim morning, the afternoon
bus ride to work, bleary-eyed, the endless hours
given over to others in the name of survival,
collapsing at night onto a musty mattress
on the floor; I remember the kindness and mercy
of the young women who passed through,
bringing canned soup and the comfort of touch, so new
and foreign, the small curtains of their mysterious
rooms opening just enough to let the light in,
remember the Dutch Bar across the street,
the line of gleaming Harleys outside, where someone
seemed to get stabbed every other week,
and the elderly deaf-mute down the hall signaling
to no one in particular, a pinched sound like
a distant bird rising from the well of her throat,
a word of caution, perhaps, or insight that
I could not understand, then or now.

# Why I Live in a Cold Climate

Because the sound of ice cracking beneath my feet reminds me of wooden ships awakening for a journey. Because that journey can be long and arduous. Because frost collecting in the corners of darkened window glass becomes a kind of map, more reliable than starlight alone. Because I always liked you in a hat, and our bodies draw sudden sparks beneath the drab woolen blankets. Because our breath here can be seen as easily as any cloud passing, our silence sent skyward along with our prayers. Because in winter we walk easily upon water, never questioning the river's current or where we might have left the shore. Because you can follow the tracks of those who have trudged through the snow before you, making a path for others yet to come. Because sound travels far in the cold, and we have learned to listen. Because the Cardinals and house finches remind us to sing, in spite of it all. Because there are as many names and varieties of snow as there are for their Creator. Because whenever you drop a glove here, a stranger will inevitably call out, saving you yet again, and your saying thank you is really an offering of love you cannot quite admit to. But you feel the warmth of that fabric once again encircling your fingers, small but undeniable, feel the pinprick ache of blood's knowing return, and that may be enough for now.

# THE MISSING FINGER

In one version of the story, your grandfather
walks purposefully through the gently rustling field,
his steps only slightly wider than usual,
his jaw clenched, his mouth pulled inward,
holding high in one hand the finger
which the shears have suddenly removed.
In the barn, the sheep wait quietly, perplexed,
half-kneeling, as if in prayer, the wine-dark blood –
not their own this time – already seeping
into the earth-damp wood and straw.
In another telling, he angles the gun barrel
as though it were another limb, one eye
closed to the world of dancing summer leaves,
of soft breezes and silent water winding
back upon itself. He is an easy target
for himself, the burnt smell of flesh strangely
familiar, as the war draft notice flutters
on the kitchen linoleum, nearly rising into flight.
No one is left now to remember, or to claim
this as anything other than family lore.
Yet in your mind's eye you can clearly see him,
his worn denim sleeve waving, urgent yet
measured, to someone in the distance,
someone his hands know as well as this land,
his face nearly concealed by the wide brim of his hat,
a passing cloud of sepia and dust moving in.
But you know it's him by what is missing,
as you would know the family member left out
of the photograph, a slash of hazy sunlight
where a body might be standing, the empty room
of that space lit up once, then again.

# Notes After a Blackout

For days – then weeks – after the fall,
when those sudden waves of dizziness would
arise with even the smallest of movements,
and turning over in bed meant pulling
the whole lopsided world up beside me
as well, I found myself practicing gassho after
a long and lazy absence – first in my
mind's eye, then placing my palms together
just above heart level, centering, centering,
denying the duality of left and right,
up and down, false gravity pulling me
in both directions at once. It surprised me,
this seemingly inadvertent reverence, as if I had
been granted a small offering of grace,
the unassuming dignity of walking slowly,
cautiously from one room to the next.
I felt in that moment a measure of kindness
toward the bruised and swollen face
gazing back from the medicine cabinet mirror –
a face that here needed neither explanation
nor apology – the same face that had
been waiting there for all this time.

# DENOMINATION BLUES

When my mother found Jesus again,
after narrowly surviving death by her own hand,
she began opening doors to seemingly every
church which may have housed him there.
She refused to recognize the Catholic church,
which placed a pope between oneself and the Lord,
praying to people and statues, while Lutherans
were simply too formal and reserved.
The Primitive Baptists believed that to enter
into the Kingdom you must also wash the feet
of others, as the Lord himself had done,
become a servant to the servant among us.
But there was no music there, and didn't
the psalms themselves command us to make
a joyful noise unto the Lord, loud enough
to be heard out there among the stars?
The Seventh Day Adventists seemed kind and
welcoming enough, but my brother and I protested
missing our Saturday morning cartoons.
What my mother truly loved, and where she felt
at home, was listening in earnest to those
fire and brimstone sermons, what she called
the old time religion, which threatened continually
the burning, lashing, and gnashing of teeth.
She would nod in agreement, strangely
comforted by the litany of righteous violence,
of Jesus returning next time with a sword.
She was happy to not be amongst those left,
waking on Judgement Day to find a world strange
and unwelcoming, hovering between life and

death, with no way then of repentance
or altering the course of all that was to come.

# Echocardiogram

There was a time, not so long ago,
when a young woman's hand sweeping
gently, purposefully across your bare chest
would spark a rush of movement
within the blood, stir the recognition
of one flesh meeting another, somehow
both new and ancient at once.
But today you have crossed a threshold
of sorts, where this young woman,
who balances perfectly kindness and business,
measures every bruised and weary chamber
of your heart. "Breathe in," she intones.
"Now stop. Hold that breath... Good."
From the corner of your eye, you can see
the black and white of the ultrasound,
like a closeup of the moon, or years ago
seeing your daughter for the first time,
hiccuping within her mother's frame.
You think, too, of the Buddha, said to pass
into prajna nibbana this way, reclined
on his left side, eyes half-closed, neither
looking nor looking away. But this,
this, you think, is merely a form of limbo,
the moment midway through the play
when the stage lights dim to a dusty blue
and the whole of the set is quickly rearranged.
You sit upright, button your shirt, surprised
by the sudden return of clinical light.
You thank her for her trouble, take the old soldier
in your chest – by turns too fast, too slow,

too big for its own good – meandering
down the hall, and out into the wintery day,
blustery and colorless, quietly resigned
to whatever might happen next.

# SNAPSHOT OF MY GRANDPARENTS, circa 1947

*for Nels and Tyyne Naatus*

They lean into each other, almost imperceptibly, as two old drunks, long familiar with one another, often will, partly out of love, partly out of habit. They wear neither their Saturday clothes nor their Sunday best, he in plaid farmer's jacket and frayed cap, her hat titled like a lazy flower to one side of her bronze-tinted hair. Their smiles look slightly weary, as if lacking the energy to rise fully above the surface. But this seems to be a moment on which they could agree – no arguments here, no shouting in the old language or the new – years before she chose the arsenic over the simplicity of sunlight, before cancer carved through him a path which no living thing could ever hope to travel. In this moment, the silence is not pointed but as gentle as the smoke which surrounds them, bringing them somehow closer, their pale eyes narrowed slightly against the light.

# THE LAST SUPPER

When Aunt Anita got word from the clinic
that the cancer was fanning outward
like a web of newly shattered glass,
and that it was, in fact, inoperable, she promptly
planned a get together for family and friends,
an informal wake that she would attend,
and which she dubbed – not without a touch
of gallows humor – her last supper.
She arrived in a ball gown, sequined and sparkling,
her long dark hair newly styled, flitting
from table to table, bar stool to bar stool,
glasses raised and clinking, remembering both
the good times and the hard times with
those she knew – and she knew nearly everyone.
She was their confidante, the keeper of their
family stories, sorrows, and secrets.
The next morning, she slipped quietly
into a coma, one long dream receding into
another, never again to open her eyes.
Born into nothing, into a town so insignificant
that no one had bothered to name it,
she left this world, nonetheless, dressed
to the nines, a benevolent ruler with
a Louisville slugger tucked beneath the photos
and the bottles along the bar, just in case.
She left, quite simply, glowing.

# Heart

I always thought I was simply too shy
for all those dances in the cavernous school
gymnasium, shadowing the tiled wall
while trying to appear casual, prickly sweat
mingled with drugstore perfume,
and the lights never quite dim enough,
young voices rising above the pulse of music,
searching out each other, everyone
seemingly too close and too far at once.
But perhaps it was you all along,
faulty timekeeper, clumsy blood hammer
building your secret rooms, nail by crooked nail.
You never listened well, that much
is for certain, never kept a steady beat,
just made it up as you went along,
always slightly ahead or behind,
daydreaming yourself nearly out of a job.
Heart, those bright-eyed teenage girls
have long since waltzed calmly into middle age,
and I am no jazz poet. Let's sing one
of the old songs tonight, something sweet
and simple, one that begins with barely
a whisper. You know the one.
Stay with me for just a while longer.

# LARRY

Larry was the name of the man that my mother
married next, somewhere between ECT treatments
and her daily regimen of pills – tall, gaunt and ruddy-faced,
simian ears that jutted forward like antennas,
or seashells, glowing translucent and red when
pierced by sunlight, tiny veins like a hundred cracks.
He mistook the marriage, I expect, for one
of love, but my mother needed him for
the much more practical task of disciplining my unruly
brother and me, which he did, following her
instructions like any low-level officer.
He was the first to fold me over a kitchen chair
and strike me, hard, then harder, and then hard enough
to dislodge me from my body, until there I was,
amazingly, watching somehow from above,
as though my own protector, keeper of a hidden
passageway deep within myself, previously unknown.
I didn't think that he was a bad man,
merely someone following orders, obedient
to a fault, perplexed, I imagined, as I was, watching,
as though this were but a poorly acted play.
Though I was, secretly, proud to have not cried,
proud to have left the body, without anyone so much
as noticing; and when I came back, having passed
their test, apologizing for my meager sins,
I didn't come back all the way. Not for them,
and not for a long time to come.

# The Corner

Another punishment from childhood,
as familiar as going to church or setting
the dishes out for dinner, was being sent to stand
in the corner, intersection of shame
and boredom, to think about what I had
or had not done, to gaze into nothing
and plan my humble route back to forgiveness.
I learned well the corners of every home
that we passed through, their particular silences,
removed from the clamor of daily routine,
the television's canned laughter, voices rising
and falling, bellowing from room to room.
I memorized the vein-like cracks spreading
through the eggshell plaster, air bubbles
beneath the paint, the fine, stray hairs
and wisps of spiderweb long since abandoned,
knew precisely where two sheets of wood
paneling came together, imperfectly,
the slender nails that held them,
and where the tiny splinters slept hidden.
I couldn't help but wonder why I disappointed
God so often, and why I seemed so far
removed from his sacred image.
I learned to sleep standing up, unnoticed,
learned to count obsessively the ceiling tiles,
the inward folds of curtains, and wallpaper patterns,
learned to turn my mind off, and on,
and off again; I became still, became a very
fine singer in the auditorium of self.
I learned, through necessity, that my place

was just off to the side, resting
on the warm shoulder of my thoughts,
and that even the smallest hint of disobedience
could send me back to windowless solitude,
and that the wrong words spoken
could bring the whole structure down.

# Searching for the Poet's Grave

They are searching for Lorca's remains again
today, their big yellow machinery
nudging and clawing at the silent earth,
scooping out rows and rows of doorways
along this withered patch of soil.

Though no one is here now to answer them,
no one to say, No thank you, sirs,
I'm not interested in returning,
and your Bible is no map for my soul.

But they have not questioned the cloud formations
in passing, nor the monuments of generals,
nor the crooked olive trees, unwaveringly lazy
in their beauty, witnesses to all.
No one has called in the sun and moon
to spit out their long and secret songs, explain
their absence when needed most.

No one has yet knocked upon my door,
demanding to peruse the shelves,
where they would surely find the one they seek,
still speaking, unafraid, his linen suit
not even wrinkled.

But the workers, naturally, will go on
with their labors, long past sunset,
coming back empty handed, the shapes of
new countries emerging through their shirt-sweat,
while the poet just goes on dreaming,

as he did a hundred years ago,
the witness to his whereabouts
now seemingly everywhere.

# Compassionate Release

My grandfather came home from state prison
hardly noticed, came home simply to die
in peace, or rather, in whatever semblance of
peace a man like him could be granted –
the memory of past sins having their final say,
while cancer gnawed slowly at his bones.
Though not slowly enough and not
painfully enough, my aunt later quipped.
On that first, and last, hospital visit
he resembled most, to my young eyes,
the Egyptian mummy sleeping under glass
at the science museum – that bleak
skeletal grimace glowing ghostly through
the centuries, one long, withered finger
pointing toward, or reaching out for,
what we could only imagine, ancient gauze
dangling like flesh in the clinical light,
the merely human drawing gasps of fear
and fascination from all of us gathered there.
I feared this husk of a man, and for him,
feared him instinctively, not quite knowing why.
My mother bent low to whisper to him
the forgiveness which her faith demanded,
as one would comfort a suffering child,
before walking us kids solemnly back
outside, the night suddenly quiet, hesitant,
the winter sky hanging flat and low
against the earth, our small breath visible,
hovering in the air between us.

# THE COUNTY LINE

Having waded through the green waves of ditch grass
and wildflowers, bramble grown nearly waist-high,

the prickly stems of young strawberries
and the private cosmology of gnats, we arrive

like casual explorers to examine the broken foundation,
hidden from view off the highway, of what once was

The County Line Bar, place where my grandparents –
only yesterday, it seems – served up libations

to the always thirsty locals and those passing through,
no doubt consuming as much as they sold.

Who's to say that these ruins are not sacred,
or that their ghosts are unworthy of remembrance?

Just over there, my grandmother stood for what has
become my favorite photograph of her, framed

on either side by my grandfather and two regulars,
laughing, girlish, and seemingly without care,

her small dog held close against her, one cloud of breath,
all but invisible, hovering in the crisp winter air.

This is how I want to remember her, her smile
like a sudden flash of daylight, the gold in her hair

shining, even in black and white – before the loss
of a son on the other side of the world severed

something in her irreparably, before the alcohol bruised
and the weight of her days became too much.

I need to remember this moment, if only for myself,
to remember that she knew joy upon this earth,

the ease and gentleness of common things,
that she loved, and was called beloved in return.

# New Kid

We moved whenever the rent increased,
which must have been quite often,
packing up our things into liquor store boxes
and garbage bags, those once-familiar
rooms swept clean, white, our voices echoing back.
Perpetually the new kid in class, slipping in
during the middle of the year, I found
a desk near the back whenever possible,
my voice hesitant and far off, as if part of it had
been left in another town, when asked to
tell the class something about myself.
How could I speak of what I did not know?
We lived sometimes with strangers, or family,
friends of friends, not quite understanding
the politics, daily routines, or household rules,
breathing the strange smell of other lives,
sometimes not bothering to fully unpack our own.
There were so many kids and so many names
that eventually I stopped learning them,
stopped asking, stopped speaking my own.
My role was that of the other, a vague curiosity,
gazing out of winter windows, taking notes.
But I learned to love, if only in passing,
to love from a greater and greater distance.
And to all those who have passed through –
so quickly, so quickly – I loved you all,
in my own peculiar way, and I can almost see
you now in my rear view, right where you've
always been, growing closer and closer
with each passing year.

# My Great-grandmother at 75

In the photo, grown cracked and distant
with age, my great-grandmother Kustaava is seated
outdoors, her plain dress dignified, unadorned,
a large birthday cake balanced on her lap.
Her face, remarkably unlined, looks on, quizzically,
head tilted slightly to one side, a thin glimmer
of a smile shining forth through shadow.
She is centered perfectly in the frame,
as she was undoubtedly in life, yet clearly seems
unaccustomed to such a fuss being made.
In the lower left, the back tire of a Model-T
casts its lengthening shadow, a tangible bridge
stretching from one century to the next;
while further off to the right, a milk pail stands
as a reminder that this life is a life of work,
its chores never finished, and that cows, chickens,
and children pay little heed to the sabbath.
But in this moment, at least, she appears content
with it all, the moment of stillness well earned.
In the next, she will draw her breath in deeply,
blow the candles out like so many sparks
of light in the night sky, out past the camera's
shuttered lens, beyond her own imagining,
far enough to find us here, still in need of such light.
Send more, *Isoaiti*, send more.

# III

# Turn Your Radio On

Walking past that small old church
on the corner today, so drab and unassuming
that you might well miss it, I stopped
to gaze up at the radio tower, its thin needle
appearing to pierce the chilly blue sky,
a steeple once lit with the living spirit,
or so we were assured as children.
I could almost hear my mother in that moment,
singing those old country hymns
across the crackling airwaves, tunes
long gone out of fashion, but reaching
out to whomever might need them.
"Get in touch with God," she would sing
in earnest, "Turn your radio on."
What strikes me now is the very absence of
song, a silence born not of reverence but
of neglect, as if the white brick and weathered
boards were sinking slowly into themselves.
Perhaps it is simply the quiet of knowing,
the calm certainty of no longer having
to meet every voice with your own.
But the old transmitter glints as brightly as ever
in the afternoon sun, reaches up toward
the heavens, as if in expectation, and the songs
that my mother once sang are now mine
and mine alone, to hum as I walk by, though
my thin voice hardly makes a sound.

# THE SOCIALIST OPERA HOUSE

It's long gone now, the place where the working class Finns once met to raise their banners and sing the songs of labor, to create upon the stage a world that made a bit more sense, and taught the lessons not yet learned. Gone now are the dirt farmers with broken English and missing fingers, the rebel girls and rabble rousers, the miners who shed their blood for a day's pay and a day of rest in this land of the free. Gone now, one dream swallowed by another when no one was looking. Though the bones of this building remain, housing yet another office, yet another bank. The stage is still there, hollow and long unused, holding close its secrets in dusty curtain folds and boards. The old songs are still there for any voice to lift again. The prop ship still hangs in the dust of darkened rafters, white sails torn and frayed, ready to set sail for a paradise, real or imagined, so very far from here.

# What We Carried with Us

It couldn't have been much, whatever
could be tossed into two plastic garbage bags
and carried, from the station wagon
to the front porch of our new foster home,

a word which we had neither heard nor spoken,
but one that would become as common
as a surname, shorthand for others to describe us.

We carried our toothbrushes and combs,
clothes and underwear, carried whatever toys
or stuffed animal could be retrieved,
while the cacophony of sirens sped our comatose
mother to the cold comfort of hospital rooms,
plastic roses, a potpourri of pills to replace
the ones which had not managed to kill her.

We took a blanket or two, worn and pilling,
superhero pajamas, damp familiarity
of our own sweat-smell.

But mostly, we took all that we could not
speak of – the unshifting weight which
an absent father leaves, ladder rungs of anxiety
we could neither climb nor give name to,
the mutual shame of bed wetting
and the sudden difficulty of common speech.

We carried each other, brother, hardly
aware that we were doing so, always balancing,
always stronger than we looked or imagined.

We carried that grief until it settled in,
quiet and unobtrusive, a gentle tune humming
through the bones. I'm singing it now, though you
have been gone now all these years,

pausing just long enough for you to whistle
through the grass blades, bend that grosbeak's note
just so, rustle the cotton shirts and work pants
upon the line in a pantomime of breath,
the familiar motion of walking away.

# THE ANIMAL PHILOSOPHER

Walking with my young daughter to school,
she asks, seemingly out of nowhere,
"What are words anyway?
They don't mean anything, really.
What is a girl, or a tree, or the ocean?
To an animal, the words we use
are just sounds like any other sound."
And I, who have spent the better part of
a lifetime believing in the beauty
and possibility of language, of building these
small temples of measured sound,
can offer no reasonable defense against
such a pure distillation of truth.
Have I been exposed as a mere hack,
I wonder, a mild-mannered charlatan? I am,
if I'm being honest, slightly wounded
by her conviction, the ease and suddenness
with which she throws out the question
of the ages. "Why are we here?
No one knows. The animals would know
because they were here long before humans.
We can't really understand their language,
but we could learn if we listened."
Which is all her father, poor simpleton,
can manage today, tagging along,
tearing up pages in the back of my mind,
the need for words between us
growing further and further away.

# COVER OF NIGHT

My mother's head leans forward with sleep,
the old station wagon veering slightly
into the next lane before righting itself,
the seemingly endless stretch of road unspooling
before us, cut only by two imperfect
cones of light. We are fleeing – there is no
other word – by cover of night,
fleeing the McDonough housing projects
and that angry mob, which had pinned
my skinny and terrified brother
against the screen door as he called out
for divine intervention or miracle of physics
that might allow him to pass through
metal, pass through wood, back into safety.
So, we are driving the long, anonymous hours,
the city already receding into memory,
replaced by ink-black trees on either side,
a deep, unfamiliar quiet running its hands
through every root and thread at once.
We travel like gypsies, with neither grace
nor guile, our childhoods rushing past
as quickly as the white lines of the highway.
In the morning, we will wake to a different world,
smell of red earth and lake water
the faint rustling of dry summer corn.
But tonight, we nod off beneath stars never
seen in the city, small pins of light
piercing through the window glass, holding up
this thin blanket of night for a few more
hours, before daylight tears it all down again.

# COMFORTING THE CHILD

Being the only son of parents who
abandoned their children as easily as one
walks to the grocery store – one
preferring the soft oblivion of Stoli and
sleeping pills, the other the peculiar balance of
status and anonymity that only money
affords, – I stand, perhaps, too closely to
my own girl, always on guard,
hovering, worrying myself into sleeplessness.
I am nothing if not vigilant, an occasional
nuisance of concern, golden retriever of a father
at the gate, barely blinking, awaiting my cue.
When she races up the steps of her school,
confident in a way which I never was,
my pride mingles with a tinge of unspoken grief.
Still, I want nothing more than to be taken
for granted, to never be known as an absence.
I want for her the autonomy of knowing,
for love to be as constant and as easily forgotten
as the silent pulse of blood at wrist
and ankle, and my hand upon her shoulder
when she hurts, drawing circles
on her back, comforting, not only her
but the child no longer there.

# THE MOON IN MY HAND

Today I held in my outstretched palm
a smooth, flat piece of moon stone,
black, ordinary, impenetrable,
nothing you would consider otherworldly,
nor containing even the smallest
fragment of mystery or light.
Nothing asking to be named or known,
merely a door opening into further darkness.
When my daughter was very small
she would exclaim in joyous wonder
from the balcony, "The moon! The moon!,"
greeting her nightly friend once again.
But this, this cannot be the moon,
I think. This is mere flint, shale, asphalt,
chimney soot swept and hardened
to a coin of no value here below.
No miner would bother to claim it.
But a child can easily see light where
our eyes cannot, can spark a new
world from nearly anything within reach.
We add our stone to the fish bowl
full of earthly ones, our own small piece
of moon, which we read has traveled
hundreds of thousands of miles
to be right here beside us, where we rest
and dream another day into waking.

# FEATHERS OF A DOVE

How many trips did we make back then
to the hardware store, as summer
leaned lazily into autumn; how many
dusky shades of blue and gray
holding their secret oceans of light
were mixed on our behalf, a seemingly
endless variety of color swatches
laid out like narrow, unframed windows,
opening onto a bright coastal morning
which no artist could ever have gotten right?
How elegant and whimsical their names,
dreamed up, I imagine, in some drab
and lifeless boardroom, and labeled here
in practiced script: English Chamomile,
Whispering Mist, Feathers of a Dove.
We read them aloud just to hear their music,
the unassuming romance they promised,
the time we longed for most of all.
How many thoughtless brushstrokes
covered the wall at the end of that narrow
hallway, as if the smallest of decisions
could make all the difference for us?
How many weeks before the baby arrived
to parents who could not agree
even on this, our days together already
beginning to flutter from our grasp, restless
and unfinished, all but flying away?

# A ROLL OF FILM

Who knows how many years it lay hidden,
slumbering in that corner of the desk drawer,
framed within its oak walls and shadow,
time slowly unspooling in either direction
around it, the constellations of dust
forming and reforming in a world which
from here must seem only a rumor.
When I retrieved them from the photo shop,
there wasn't much to see – shapeless
clusters of dark and light merging uneasily,
bursts of summer sun breaking through,
or what might have been a face, or a shoulder,
impossible to distinguish one from the other.
This is the way of all memory, I imagine.
But one image survived to show you,
standing in the doorway, your back turned
to the camera, that long black coat
concealing your frame, Christmas lights
on the tree blurred as if in motion.
I like to think you were smiling, your unshaven
face tilted slightly to one side, half hidden,
your secrets, as always, held closely.
From this distance, it is impossible to tell
if you were leaving or just arriving,
so fitting for you, brother, who could not
stay here long, but waited patiently
until today to pass through once more.

# MATHEMATICS

My scalp prickled with tiny beads of anxiety. Everyone had left school but me, and Mr. Heaney, who hovered like an unwelcome shadow, rising occasionally from his desk, his New Balance sneakers silent in their slow, measured steps. The blackboard had been wiped clean, dark as the night sky, only a few ghostly wisps of another world showing through. I was trying and failing, trying and failing, at long division, the paper wearing through from my endless corrections. "The universe is made of numbers," I was told again and again. "You must know this, if you are to know anything." I did not doubt this, though it was a language the Creator had somehow chosen to keep from me. I labored on as the afternoon light gradually shifted, and the clock ticked out its seconds, each with a small sense of finality. I could imagine the invisible threads connecting all things, though I gave them neither name nor meaning. I could hear the voices of summer outside rising and falling, could almost make out the words that elicited their sudden laughter, though it all seemed, in those moments, to be light years away.

# In the Absence of

Lately, my daughter has been having brief episodes of leaving this world. What were once generally referred to as spells. Or perhaps, it is the world that is turning away, walking past her periphery and into nothingness. The world of things simply needing a moment to collect itself. The world of images suddenly with nothing new to offer. Perhaps she is discovering, as she must, that the universe is made mostly of absence, that form is yet another emptiness, and emptiness that which we perceive as form. "Just now," she says, "when I was talking to you, for a minute I couldn't see or hear you." "But I was right here," I remind her, "Even when you thought I had gone away." I want her to remember this, many years from now, want her to rest easy in the absence I have created solely for her.

# Dearest Bully

I can still feel the rap of your knuckles,
brother, striking against my own,
stinging, bruising, like four faceless
skulls declaring their dominance.
I can still feel the weighted air shifting
between us, I who was never quite
quick enough to slip from beneath your
reach, and rarely, if ever, managed to connect.
There are things I cannot pretend
to miss – the swift punch to the shoulder,
the ever-elaborate wrestling holds,
a perfect pearl of milky spit dangling,
like a lazy thought, above my face.
I do not miss the ghost you pretended
to be, silent, tugging, inch by creeping inch,
at the foot of our childhood bed.
Your ghost is real now, free to wander
room to room. And I no longer fear,
though the world you left compels us to.
I miss you in the ways you were soft,
the gentle humor you held close,
the vulnerable boy hidden from view.
I miss the moments you cried, unashamed.
Tonight, as always, I kiss my daughter,
let her snuggle in, as she wraps her
small fingers around my crooked thumb,
drifting effortlessly again into sleep.
It's the kind of calm that I live for,
and would fight this whole world to keep.

# SENSITIVE

I never wanted for you, dearest daughter,
to be anything other than the beautiful and sensitive

soul you have always been, collecting oak seeds
to watch them spin back to the earth,

those long-stemmed dandelions bent over as if in prayer,
deciphering the forms of strange new animals

among the clouds, where the ancestors sleep,
faces smiling back from the most ordinary of stone.

I have admired, as an outsider, the special language
you share with birds and trees, how the cats

in the neighborhood all come to you, unafraid,,
knowing you already, and how you mourned deeply

the death of your betta fish, the one you called
your sister and confided your worries to.

I have heard you choosing each word for a poem
or song, tapping them against the roof

of your mouth, letting the new sounds settle,
until they filled your ears as perfectly as the silence,

watched you conduct, with arms gently waving,
a string concerto constructed in your mind;

and when bullies have thrown their sharpened words
like so many stones, I have sat within your sorrow,

unable to offer an answer as to why some, young
or old, simply enjoy the act of causing harm.

These are the times when I want nothing more than to
protect you from the inclement weather of self,

the ever-shifting weather of your inner world
overwhelming you, to close, temporarily, the windows

against the sudden rain of summer, until the sun
again finds its way, small enough to tuck into

your pocket like a coin, thin and hot to the touch,
rubbed smooth at the center, reflecting.

# At the Naturalization Ceremony

The families begin arriving early, the men in freshly
pressed suits, pocket squares, the women in bold patterned
dresses and colors that defy the gray drizzling skies,
their faces without exception beaming with light,
young children at their sides looking up,
knowing this day to be something extraordinary.
"There are people who live here who hate this country,"
the young woman from Colombia explains
to a local newscaster, shaking her head, "but to us,
this is still The Promised Land. It's everything."
I can't help but think of my own ancestors, who, too,
arrived with nothing, learned to speak this strange, unruly
language, drive cars, fight this nation's many wars.
It's hard to imagine my steely-eyed great grandfather,
never caught smiling in a photo, wearing a face of
such unabashed joy. But what do I know of another's heart?
I know only this moment, this day, this swell of pride
as these new citizens make their way up Kellogg Boulevard,
their small flags waving in the chilly damp air.
It is as though a hundred or more makeshift boats were
setting out, each on a separate but similar course.
Even when they have all but vanished from view,
their voices can still be heard singing, laughing,
proclaiming – so many different dialects, different
songs, so many different ways to say Home.

# Baptism

The preacher pinches my nostrils between
thumb and forefinger, pushes me
backward, hard, into the chlorine sting
of the pool, its deep, still water immediately
closing in around me like a second flesh,
heavy and resolute. Once, then again,
I go under, the former self of my childhood
swimming away, an embryo in reverse.
The age of reason, against every obstacle,
has found me. I am old enough now,
my mother reminds me, to be held accountable,
old enough to suffer those unrelenting
flames through eternity, for lack of belief,
unintended blasphemy, or simple understanding.
Far overhead, the sun blazes on, unblinking,
the world surrounding it seemingly
turning upside down, wheeling, tumbling,
while here below, sudden slashes
of light pierce my uncertain periphery.
My instinct is to reach for it, to kick, flail,
break away; my instinct is to save
myself, to simply not drown – as I feel I am –
whether by water, wine, or blood of the lamb.
Then, as if it were unexpected, I am
pulled back into the world, sputtering, gasping,
the welcome shock of oxygen like pinpricks
to the lungs, as if I had been running for miles,
my first steps back on land uncertain.
This world is not my home, they are singing,
so happy to only be passing through.

But I don't know what could be better than
this – the earth that accepts us again
and again, sinners to the last,
the one on which we write our songs, the one
that sings them back to us in return.

# Acknowledgements

"Storm," "Candy Cigarettes," "The Buggy," "My Daughter Speaks of Birds," "All the Love We Lay Claim to," "Sensitive," "At the Naturalization Ceremony," and "Baptism" previously appeared in *Autumn Sky Poetry Daily*.

"D.A.V. Thrift Store," and "Mother and Child" previously appeared in *Red Eft Review*.

"Cousteau" previously appeared in *Boomer Lit Mag*.

"Why I Live in a Cold Climate" previously appeared in *Fantastic Imaginary Creatures: An Anthology of Contemporary Prose Poems* (Madville Publishing).

"Candy Cigarettes" was nominated for a Pushcart Prize.

"Baptism" was nominated for Best of the Net 2023.

Special thanks to Susanne Maldonado for her helpful suggestions on the arrangement of these poems.

# About the Author

GREG WATSON's work has appeared widely in various journals and anthologies, and has been nominated for both the Pushcart Prize and Best of the Net. He is the author of nine collections of poetry, most recently *The Sound of Light*, published by Whistling Shade Press. He is also co-editor with Richard Broderick of *The Road by Heart: Poems of Fatherhood*, published by Nodin Press. He lives in Saint Paul, Minnesota.

For more information, please visit *www.gregwatsonpoet.com*